Ebook covers

HOW TO MAKE EBOOK COVERS EASILY

BY

KATHLEEN MORRIS

Rouge Publishing

Rouge Publishing

978-1927828113

Other Books By Kathleen Morris

<u>Deep Bay Series</u>
Deep Bay Vengeance
Deep Bay Relic
Deep Bay Legacy (Coming 2014)

<u>Blood War Series</u>
The Prion Attachment
Blood Purge (Coming 2014)

<u>Short Inspirations Series</u>
Size Seven Shorts
Short End Of The Stick
Shortcut To Alaska

<u>Short Stories</u>
Along The Way - 12 Short Stories You Can Read Along
The Way

<u>Plays</u>
Time Will Tell - An Easter Play
Even Me - A Christmas Play For Your Sunday School
All I Need Is Love - A Play For Teens
Lost And Found - A Children's Christmas Play
Gotta Love It - A Humorous Play About Rural Life

<u>How - To Books</u>
How To Make Eye Catching Ebook Covers Easily

Available on Amazon.com

DEDICATION

...for my mother

TABLE OF CONTENTS

INTRODUCTION

You don't need to be a professional to make your own ebook covers, and you don't need to spend a fortune on ebook making software to do it. All you need is a digital camera and a way to edit your pictures. You don't need to be a professional photographer, and you don't need to be a graphic artist to do this either.

In the following chapters, I'll reveal what I do to make ebook covers and you don't have to spend a small fortune on a quality digital camera or high end photo editing software. You can do this on a shoestring budget in very little time. It won't look amateurish and it will be fairly simple to do.

Most people know how to use a digital camera anyway, and we already have some way to load our pictures onto photo editing software already on our computer. If you take pictures for Christmas, birthdays, or major events in your life, you already know the basics in making an ebook cover.

I'll show you that making ebook covers isn't as complicated or expensive as people might think. In the following chapters, I'll show you a few tricks that I do, and hope that you too can make professional looking, eye-catching ebook covers, easily!

CHAPTER 1

TOOLS

DIGITAL CAMERAS

You don't need anything fancy like a $3000 camera or anything, just a basic digital camera will do. The kind I use is a *Canon A720 Power Shot*. It's not the newest camera, and it's probably about five years old, but it does the job and I'll tell you why.

This particular camera is only an *8 mega pixel* and you'd think with today's technology your camera has to be better than that, but it doesn't. It also has *6 times optical zoom*, but I rarely use that for ebook covers anyway.

I got my husband a brand new *Sony 16 Times Optical Zoom HD Movie 720 P Cyprus Shot* camera thinking it's the top-of-the-line and I'll start using that with my ebook covers. I might some day, but I find it too complicated. I like simple. And I think a lot of other people do as well. It's when we start getting into complicated features on the digital camera that we start losing sight of the goal. We

11

want to make an ebook cover as quickly and easily as possible, yet have it look professional enough to catch the eye of millions of readers so they download our ebooks. I don't want to spend weeks and months and possibly years perfecting an ebook cover when I don't have to.

PHOTOGRAPHY EDITING SOFTWARE

There are many different kinds of photo editing software, and you can spend a great deal of money on them, and time researching and learning how to use them. You don't have to. I fell into this trap and spent a small fortune on *Lightroom 4*. Don't get me wrong, it's amazing - if you can figure it out. It's very complicated and requires a lot of time learning technical terms, and what they mean. And it doesn't come with a manual either. I had to watch YouTube videos just to figure the whole thing out, and there is still so much I don't know about the software.

I actually love my *Lightroom 4*, but seldom use all the special features. I prefer to edit lighting and shadows only, in this software, because I don't want to spend all day mucking around with the technical aspect of it. There's also an ad-on feature to *Lightroom 4* as well that you can utilize. I added on *Perfect Layers* from *onOne* so that I could layer pictures if I wanted to. That in itself was pretty complicated to figure out. When I originally bought *Lightroom 4*, I was fooled into thinking that it already had it's own layering feature. It didn't. I guess that's why you need to read the fine print.

Lightroom 4 is just one of the many photo editing software programs I use, but it doesn't have to be that complicated or expensive. You could use one basic software program and it would be just fine.

I always fall back on my old and faithful photo editing software. I purchased it over ten years ago and it's almost obsolete now, but I don't care. My *Microsoft Picture It* is something I'm familiar with and comfortable using. In its day, it was the leading photo editing software. I got to know it pretty well in the last decade and it's become like an old friend to me. If you have old photo editing software, you can still use it. Special effects are over rated anyway, and that is what draws you into buying the new software. You don't need it. It's nice to have if you want to play around with your picture, but it certainly isn't a prerequisite for making an ebook cover.

There are many free photo editing software programs you can download that will edit photos quite nicely. You don't have to go out and purchase one like I did. The absolute best free photo editing software out there right now is called *Gimp*. I have that as well, and it's awesome. Compared to *Lightroom 4* and *Perfect Layers*, it is pretty equal. You can edit a photo quite easily, change lighting, shadows, colors, layers, you name it. You can even do special effects and insert fonts for your title. I still like *Picture It* for inserting the titles but that's just me.

As I said before, *Gimp* can be downloaded and used for free. You don't need to pay a dime for it, and it's all you need to edit your photos to make an ebook cover.

There are many other free photo editing software programs as well. I'll just briefly mention the top programs. You can investigate which one is right for you. The main thing is that you don't have to pay for high quality photo editing programs to make a professional eye catching ebook cover. Here is a list of free programs: *Paint.Net*, *PhoXo*, *Funny Photo Maker*, *Photo Pos Pro*, *PhotoScape*, *Irfan View*, *PhotoFiltre*, *Pix Builder Studio*, and *Chasys Draw IES*. You can google any of these for more information on them.

There's also a program already built into your computer that will allow you to do basic photo editing. Not many people know this but it's called *Paint*. If you type it into your search bar at the bottom of your computer screen, it will pop up. I use this program only to change my pixel size so that it meets the requirements for an ebook cover. Those requirements are a standard 1600 x 2400 pixel size as outlined in the *Smashwords* guide. But it also fits quite nicely into *Kindle* uploads to Amazon. I chose to standardize my ebook covers to the *Smashwords* guidelines because *Smashwords* is the largest ebook distributor in the world, and distributes to *Apple, Kobo, Barnes & Noble*, and many other ebook stores, so you want to get the size right so your book won't get rejected for improper cover size.

CHAPTER 2

REQUIREMENTS

No matter what type of digital camera you use, or what type of photo editing software you prefer, it all means nothing without a proper photo. You always have to start with a photo and that's a problem for some people. I just want to say that it really shouldn't be a problem. People just tend to make it into one.

First you're told you have to purchase a photo from internet sites that sell them. You might look into it like I did, and then read the fine print. You don't own the picture. You'll never own the picture. Anyone else can use it. It's not exclusive to your ebook cover either. What happens if someone else makes an ebook cover with the same exact photo? That's silly, or at least I thought so. And you do have to pay a fee, even if it says it's a free stock photo. Read the fine print and who holds the copyright, and the stipulations of its use. This method is not for everyone. I wouldn't want to break any copyright laws. Heaven forbid I land in jail for something like this. But seriously, it is something we authors are concerned about whether we admit it or not. And why add insult to injury, just take your own darn photos. You'll hold the copyright then, and there won't be duplicates popping up everywhere.

My method of making ebook covers is not that risky. I simply take my own photos and work with them. With a little effort and know-how, you can too. There are a few key factors that you must consider before you snap that picture. But mark my words, regardless of the fancy camera you have or the photo editing software you think will make you good ebook covers, you first must start with a basic photo. Without that, you won't be able to make an ebook cover at all.

So here's how to get one.

A CREATIVE EYE

Not everyone is artistic and can spot a good photo when they see one. But don't let that hold you back from taking the shot. Sometimes we don't realize that we have hidden talent, and sometimes we just don't try.

My bit of advice is to be bold. Just try. You might surprise yourself with what you can come up with.

Firstly, when I'm starting to look for images I can photograph for an ebook cover, I usually don't do it until I'm completely finished writing and editing my novel. I do that because I just like to see the full picture of what the novel is about first, before I decide to represent it with an image.

And representing it with an image, is actually what we're doing.

Ask yourself what one thing would represent your story. Is it a spider in a web? Is it a gun, binoculars, a cross? These are the questions that I ask myself before I even start photographing images for an ebook cover.

You have to look at the world differently. Not as a whole; not as a big picture, but tiny little things that make it up. If we just look at a normal photograph of a prairie scene for example, it wouldn't be as effective for an ebook cover as a crooked tree in the middle of a canola field. We might want to focus on just that tree, or its branch, with only a small clip of the prairie showing in the corner of the photograph.

That's just an example, but I wanted to show you the importance of seeing the world through a writers eye, and focus on one or two particular objects that can be photographed close-up, for an ebook cover.

And my favourite secret in creating photos for ebook covers, is that most photos are flukes. Yes, you heard me right. Flukes! You don't have to be the best photographer in the world to make your own ebook cover, you just have to experiment. Which brings me to my next point.

PROPS

Sometimes what you want to take a picture of, isn't what you *should* take a picture of. Taking pictures of nature for example, might be too big for an ebook cover even if your book is about that, but the secret lies within that realm.

By that, I mean experiment with a stone for example, or a piece of jewellery, or small figurine, or even a blade of grass. Sometimes you have to take two or three objects that represent your story and lay them out for a photo shoot instead of taking that full nature shot. You might want to photograph a gun because it represents your crime novel. You might want to lay it out on a piece of colorful silk with some diamonds to represent your story about diamond smuggling. And once you have your props set up for a photo shoot, take a series of pictures, over and over, experimenting once again.

I think the most profound prop would have to be a live subject though. Ever try modelling or watching a model in a photo shoot? It's quite fascinating. We use models for their hands, feet, face, and other parts of the body. Why not use your own hand in a creative way? Why not ask a photogenic friend to pose for a profile for your romance novel? I know many people who like to dress up in costume to be photographed. Professional photographers do this all the time and they're paid big bucks to do it.

If you want to, you can pay a friend to model for you, or work out a deal where they can use your photos to build their modelling portfolio. And once people see your ebook cover with your friend's picture on it, that free exposure could quite possibly boost your friends modeling career. The opportunities are endless. You can paint a face and focus on just the eye, or do a sideways profile of a woman in a wedding gown on a windy day for your historical romance novel. It only takes imagination, and you already have *that* or you wouldn't be a writer.

There are many kinds of props, and they can do wonders for an ebook cover, but they work hand-in-hand with lighting. It's something I discovered right away, and something that adds to a photograph like nothing else.

CREATIVE LIGHTING

You can take all the pictures in the world and they would be boring without light. I try to find little beams of light cascading through my windows, and place objects there. I set up props in the light whenever I can, to create unique photos. You might be surprised what kinds of shadows pop up that you didn't realize were there.

Natural light works better than artificial light, so if you can take pictures outside and use the sun, it will give a clear crisper picture. I only take pictures inside if I can utilize natural light coming through my window. We have a skylight in our home and often the sun shines through to the kitchen countertop. I have placed many a prop on my kitchen countertop, making full use of the light.

CHAPTER 3
TECHNIQUES

In this chapter I want to focus on the many different techniques I use to create a photo for an ebook cover. Everyone is different in how they express their creativity, and there is nothing wrong with that, but I just want to shed some light on what I use.

MACRO ECONOMICS

Does that word scare you? Don't let it. It's not a photography term, just my own pun. But there are so many different photography terms that would make the novice photographer shudder. I think sometimes people like to use big words to make others seem smaller than them. You can't let yourself be intimidated by what others think, say, or do. You may know a professional photographer that would laugh at you for even trying to do your own ebook covers. They like to quickly point out that you're not experienced enough or don't have the qualifications. But you have to get passed that to make your own ebook covers. Most people don't know how to do something because they just haven't tried, or muscled up the nerve to give it a go.

It takes arrogance to do this, but there's good and bad arrogance. I just tell myself that arrogance is another term for self-confidence. All writers are arrogant in some way or another. If we weren't arrogant we would never become published authors. We simply wouldn't have the confidence to market our work and persevere through the endless obstacles in our way. We'd be too shy and insecure to even try. So, with that said, since you are arrogant like me, why not take it one step further and be arrogant enough to make your own ebook cover? You obviously got what it takes!

All you need to know is a few basic things. You don't need to know how to work every feature of your camera like the professionals do. Just the *Macro* feature. That is the *ONLY* feature I use. Yes, a photographer may laugh at you, but so what. This feature is pretty basic to use and basic is all you need.

Macro is the feature I use to take close up pictures. I don't use zoom for ebook covers, and I don't take just a normal picture, it's always in *Macro*. If you don't know where this feature is on your camera, I'd suggest you get out your camera's instruction booklet and find it immediately, because it's all you'll ever need.

Macro allows you to take close up pictures without being blurry. I've taken pictures for ebook covers without being in *Macro* and when you blow them up, they are never as crisp and clear as in *Macro*.

I find that the key to eye-catching ebook covers is taking pictures close up. Forget about the panoramic view, focus on just one or two things and take multiple pictures close up with *Macro*. They won't be blurry. I've seen professional ebook covers that were blurry and they looked juvenile to me. It's not hard to take a clear picture even close up if you turn your camera to the *Macro* setting.

Not all ereaders are the same. If you have a *Kobo* like me, you won't really notice if an ebook cover is slightly blurred. But if you use an *iPad*, you can notice a blurry ebook cover right away. It's just unattractive and unprofessional, yet I've seen and read many a professional ebook that has a blurry cover. The high-tech screen resolution of an *iPad* and many other tablets these days require clearly-focused, high-quality ebook covers. It's just the way it is. My *Kobo* isn't in color, I wish it was, but even though it's black and white, I can usually spot a poor ebook cover. I end up not reading it when the cover doesn't pull me in. It shouldn't bother me, but it does. And if it bothers me, it bothers others. We are visual people and *THAT* is what snags the reader, so make your ebook cover clear, not blurry, or people won't buy it.

Macro Economics, see! Not as hard as you thought!

USING THE PAINT FEATURE

As I mentioned before, all computers have what's called a *Paint* feature built right into the operating system. I utilize this feature to change the size of my ebook cover to the specs required but *Amazon* and *Smashwords*. If you click on the search icon on your computer and type in *Paint*, you'll find the feature that I'm talking about.

Once you open the *Paint* feature, in the far left-hand corner at the top of the screen, you'll find what looks like a little book or a pad of paper. It's a icon to represent files. What you want to do is click on the arrow and select *'open files'*. It will open to your pictures immediately and you simply select the picture that you want to resize.

At this time, you will have your ebook cover completely finished and already have the inserted fonts set into the picture for the title. You'll have already saved it into your picture files as well, so that you can utilize it through the *Paint* feature. Remember that any type of photo editing software will do the same thing, but I just prefer to use *Paint* for sizing.

Once you select the proper photo, which you *already* edited and completed for your ebook cover, you can open it and it will pop right in to the *Paint* viewer screen. Once it's in the *Paint* viewer screen, you are then free to resize it to the recommendations your ebook cover must be uploaded in.

As I said before, I follow the guidelines for *Smashwords* which is a recommended size of approximately 1600 pixels wide by 2400 pixels tall because most paperback books are that size. I just save the file in *JPEG* for *Amazon* and *PNG* for *Smashwords* because *PNG* uploads easier for *Smashwords*.

Don't be afraid to try different sizes with your picture. Once your ebook cover is inside the *Paint* viewer screen, click the resize button at the top and a new pop-up screen will come up showing you the horizontal and vertical. The amount of 100 will be in both the horizontal and vertical. What you want to do is change the horizontal, and the vertical will follow.

When your ebook cover first shows up in the *Paint* viewer screen, the sizing of that raw photo is usually 1200 x 1600. From that, you know that you must make it bigger in order for it to meet the requirements of an ebook cover. So, what you want to do is change the horizontal from 100 to 150. Automatically it will resize and show you at the bottom of the screen that it's now 1800 x 2400. Now, you can actually use the photograph for an ebook cover when it's 1800 x 2400 but I find that it's a little too wide. I have used this sizing before but I find that if I take it down just a little bit, it looks much better.

To resize it further, you need to click resize again. Take the checkmark out of '*main size ratio*' and then remove the 100 from horizontal and put in 90 instead. This will leave your vertical at 2400. We don't want to touch that. But it will adjust your horizontal slightly less, giving you the dimensions of 1620 x 2400 which fits nicely into the category required by *Smashwords*. I chose 1620, being 20 px over the limit for the horizontal, because I find that giving it that extra bit of width just looks better to me.

Once you have the proper dimensions, click the down arrow in the top left-hand screen where the book icon is, and another drop-down screen will come up asking you what you want to do. What you want to do, is scroll down to '*save as*' and to the right of the screen. The computer will ask you what you want to save it as.

Once again, I select *JPEG* for *Amazon*, then specify that it's for *Amazon* in my filename and click save. It will save in an external file in your pictures. Then I go back to *Paint* and repeat. This time I save it in *PNG* for *Smashwords* and I specify that in my filename, click and save. You can also do *Smashwords* covers in *JPEG*. I just find that the titles don't look as sharp in *JPEG*.

At that point, the ebook cover is completely done and ready to upload.

PHOTOGRAPHING IN LAYERS OR LAYERING PICTURES

These are actually two different things. Firstly, when I consider taking a picture for an ebook cover, I plan my layout. In my first book, *Deep Bay Vengeance*, I chose a gun, and some money on a blue silk background. It's a suspense, mystery and I thought it fit the story quite nicely. This ebook cover didn't require any editing at all. Yes, you heard me right. I didn't have to change the color, or the lighting, or the shadows. It was an original raw photo. All I did was add my name and a title.

Take a look at the final cover.

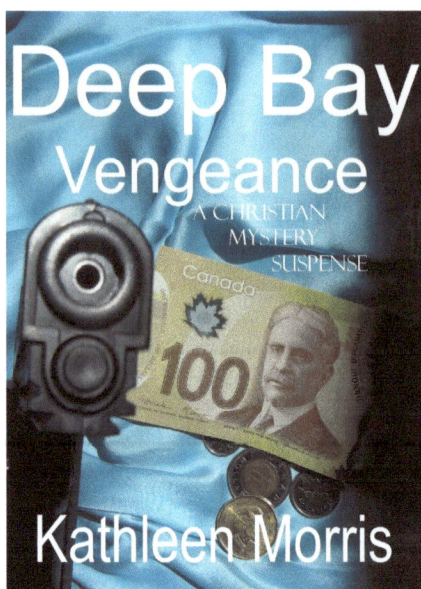

So you *can* do this!

If I can do it, so can you. All you need to do is try. If you want to bypass all that editing, you certainly can. Just snap a good picture. As I said before, I placed a gun on top of silk fabric with a one hundred dollar bill (Canadian) and made sure I strategically placed it in a beam of sunlight coming through my skylight. It was actually the sunlight that made the whole picture, not the props that I used. The sunlight just hit is perfectly.

Now, I didn't get this shot on my first try, so don't think it's that easy. It took several shots, and several different poses before I saw this beauty in the viewfinder. Seriously, it does take a bit of patience and trial and error to come up with the perfect shot. You should've seen the many other samples I took for this ebook cover. Most of them were duds, believe me. Just work at it a bit. You'll find that most of the good pictures are flukes anyway. And...if you are intimidated with the whole editing process, just layer your photo so it's all-in-one. It *can* be done!

Now, layering two pictures together is a whole different ball game. If you want to play around with editing you can layer. I've done a few ebook covers this way and it gives great results, but it requires educating yourself with the specific photo editing software you have. I wouldn't recommend starting with layering two photos, but it's up to you.

I would only layer two pictures together if it served a purpose. Sometimes it suits the ebook better, and sometimes there are technical reasons for wanting to merge a picture together. We'll go into more detail later with an example of those reasons but for now, I just want to let you know that you don't need any fancy software to layer two or more pictures together. I use *Lightroom 4* with *Perfect Layers* as an add-on but the free *Gimp* software can do the same thing without you having to pay a dime.

In conclusion, you just have to find what works for you. If you're not comfortable playing around with photo editing software, you really don't have to. If you want to, that's fine too. Just don't spend an arm and a leg purchasing expensive programs when you get the same thing with free photo editing software programs.

And please, don't frustrate yourself trying to learn every aspect of your photo editing software. Yes, you have to understand how to use the basic features, but don't make yourself crazy. The harder you make it, the harder it will be. I always refer to it as a simple kiss: Keep is simple stupid.

CHAPTER 4

COLOR

By using samples in this ebook, I hope to help those who would like a point-by-point tutorial on how I did my ebook covers. Whenever I'm asked how I did my covers, I always reply by saying it's easy. But I realize it's not easy for everyone, so I would like to use a few selected covers of my own to show you how I did it.

The first ebook cover I would like to use is called *Size Seven Shorts*. Now for this particular ebook, I didn't really know what I would use for the cover because it's a collection of seven short stories. As I thought about it, I realized I wanted to make a play on the word shorts. I thought it was fitting. I thought there was humor in it, and overall it was something that I could do quite easily.

I basically started with a pair of shorts. First, I put them on and took a picture of myself. It didn't turn out well even though I tried several different lighting techniques both with inside lighting and out. It just didn't look right to me. It looked juvenile, and when a picture looks juvenile, or fake, or staged, it will look that way to a potential buyer. Those are the ebook covers that people overlook. Don't be one of them.

The key is to do a photo shoot. I always say you have to behave your way to success, so even if you're not a seasoned photographer, or the most artistic person, you can certainly click a button. And I say click away. Do as many different poses as you can, use as many different props as you can find, and let the common denominator be something that represents your story. For me, shorts, or the play on the word shorts, represented what I had to offer in my book. It happens to be a free book in some ebook stores, but even if it's free, if it's not attractive and doesn't catch the eye of the reader, nobody will download it.

So I had my work cut out for me. I found that if I took off my shorts, and lay them on the ground, and took a picture of them up close in *Macro*, it began to look alive. I knew as soon as I saw it, that it was the picture I wanted to work with.

SAMPLE 1

CHANGING COLOR MATTERS

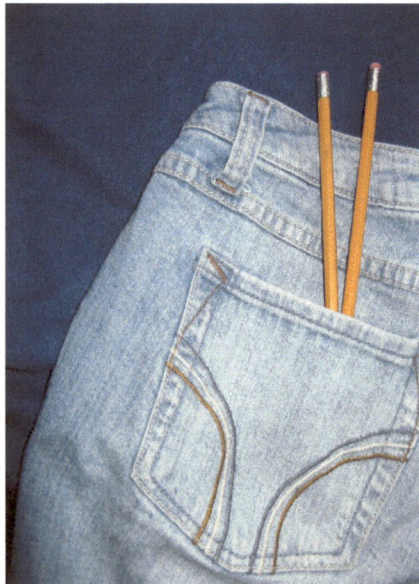

As you can see from the picture above, I laid a pair of shorts on a blue blanket on the floor, made sure my camera was in *Macro* and took a picture of it, using inside lighting from my front-room window. The pencils were like icing on the cake. They just fit.

I felt I needed to lighten the photo a bit, so I put it directly into *Picture It*, and just tried changing the coloring (hue and saturation) a little bit. I did that by adding more of a green tone to it, and automatically the stitches turned to hot pink. This caught my eye immediately and I decided to go with the hot pink because it also turned the pencils hot pink. And, I figured what caught my eye, would catch someone else's eye, giving me that eye-catching ebook cover, easily.

I added the title of the book as if it were something that was sewn right into the pocket, and offset my name with an opposite color, allowing it to stand out. I played around with different fonts as I usually do, and there really isn't a trick to choosing the best font. I find that there is no such thing as 'the best font' because it all depends on the picture you choose for your ebook cover.

I play around with the fonts and save several different samples with different fonts. I save them in a separate file and then leave them overnight. When I come back to them the next morning, I can usually pinpoint the ones that are not going to work, and the ones that will. I look at the thumbnail size, and also zoom it bigger to make sure it's not blurry.

Sometimes there's a space open in the photo where words just naturally fit. I try to utilize those spaces and balance the photo with words.

For *Size Seven Shorts,* all I had to do was change the color of the photo, and it all came together. Some photos, I've had to play around with it in *Lightroom 4* first, changing the shadows and the light, then inserting the title.

Here is the finished photo of the book cover.

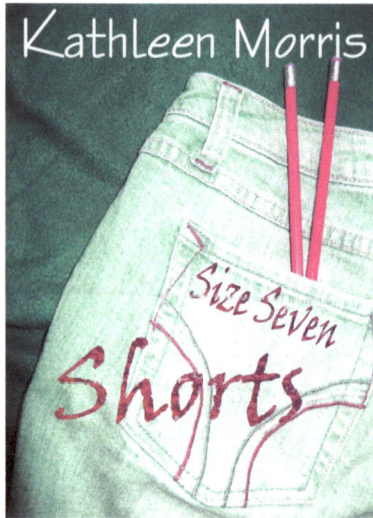

As you can see, the green brought out the hot pink, and the hot pink title worked well with it. There was an empty gap at the top of the picture, which presented itself as a natural place to put my name. If you can see the number seven in the sewing on the pocket, then you have a keen eye for detail. I noticed it right away, and thought that was eye-catching. Notice how it looks like 'size seven' is sown right into the pocket.

I created this ebook with just my camera and it didn't cost me a dime. I didn't have to use specialized ebook making software. I didn't have to pay an arm and a leg to a graphic artist either, and I own the copyright. It only took me a couple of days from start to finish, and that's not bad considering it takes graphic artists much longer to do the same thing.

SAMPLE 2

YOU DON'T ALWAYS NEED A LIVE SUBJECT

I have a few children's plays published, and one might think that the cover for a play wouldn't be as important. On the contrary. If it doesn't have an eye-catching ebook cover, once again people will bypass it. Even something as simple as a children's play needs to have an attractive ebook cover. Because after all, people download it for an reader, or print it out in *PDF*. If it's unattractive, it just won't be sellable.

The ebook cover for my play was a little bit more of a challenge. I didn't know if I should use a live subject, or take a picture of a barn, or what I should do. The play is called, *Lost And Found - A Children's Christmas Play*. I wanted to photograph a stable maybe, or hay, or some kind of nativity scene, but I also wanted it to represent what the play was about and that was the traditional nativity scene with Mary and Joseph, and barn animals.

At first I attempted to take a picture of my own profile, draping a blue sheet over my head as a silhouette of Mary. Now that was a laugh, because when I looked at the picture I realized I was much too old to be Mary, and it simply didn't look right so I scrapped it. You might have to do that once in a while. Just be brave, be daring, and take pictures of things you never would otherwise, even if people call you strange.

I moved on to a little plastic stable with figurines that we set up under a Christmas tree every year. I thought if I took a picture of that, it would look like a stable, but all it looked like was a silly toy. It looked very fake to me. Once again, if it looks fake to you, it will look fake to others, and it won't be eye-catching enough to bring in sales.

I moved on to my next idea. I really wanted a picture of Mary, but I didn't want to buy a photo, or infringe copyright laws by stealing a picture on the Internet. This is a big no-no. You need a license if you want to use someone else's photo for an ebook cover. Owning the copyright is a must no matter what anyone says. It's the law!

I decided I would use an antique plastic figurine I had of Mary. We put her in the nativity scene under our tree every Christmas. I didn't want to take a picture of just the plastic figurine though, because it looked very fake. I wanted to use it in a unique way, and possibly play around with lighting and shadows.

I took the picture of the figurine against the sky, against the sun, against the trees, and in many different lighting situations. It took a lot of trial and error before I found the one I knew I wanted to use. And remember, once again, you have to take it in *Macro* setting or it will be blurry.

This is what I came up with.

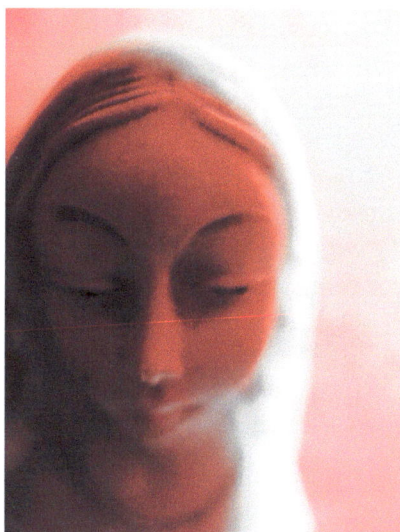

This particular picture evolved from holding the figurine in the sun against the sky believe it or not. The sun hit it in such a way that brought red into the picture. I did alter the shadow slightly in this picture above, because I was playing around with it in *Lightroom 4* and lost the original. But it's near exact to what it appeared to be in the camera viewfinder, minus the dark grey area in the corner.

Now in this picture, you see Mary is almost like a silhouette. I thought that the red was very fitting for Christmas too. And I had to admit, Mary looked way younger than I ever could. A much better model. There were also a lot of blank spaces that I figured I could use for the title as well.

So I continued to alter the color in *Lightroom 4* and decided it was just too dark as a thumbnail. I wanted people to actually be able to see what the picture was so I lightened it up and added text, and put a creative cross in the center of Mary's forehead to go with the title.

Here is the final ebook cover.

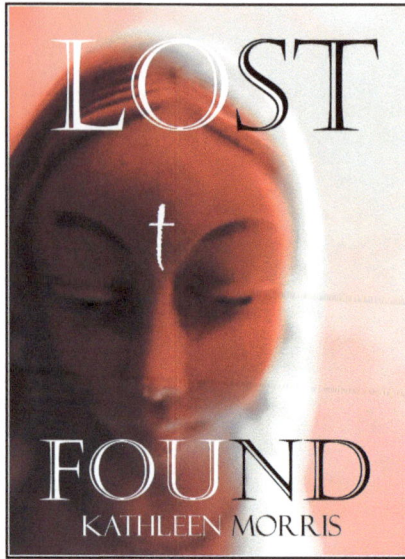

Another thing I added to this particular ebook cover, was a border. Sometimes you might need to add borders to photos so they don't look like a photo. It's funny because it's a photo, and everybody knows it, but it's also an ebook cover. The way I added the border was through *Picture It*. It has a setting that allows you to add it through clicking *effects*, then *edges*, and then *borders*. But depending on your specific software, every program is different. Just learn your specific software and understand the basic workings of it, and you can do the same thing.

In conclusion, I just wanted to point out that you can use almost any prop for an ebook cover, even a childlike figurine. You just have to be creative with lighting and shadows and play with color. It's all really as simple as that.

CHAPTER 5

USE WHAT YOU'VE GOT

SAMPLE 1

PROPS IN THE SHOP

This next sample has to be one of my favourite ebook covers. And this one is a play as well. When I first started taking pictures of things I wanted to represent this particular play, I wanted to find something that represented rural life because the play was about that. Basically it's a play about moving into an old fixer-upper farm house.

I decided I wanted to take pictures of tools in my husband's shop. I had never done that before and wondered what I could possibly find there that would create an eye-catching ebook cover. It was unorthodox, but I asked myself why not. After all, it wasn't *what* I photographed, but *how*.

I took pictures of hammers, and nails, and old broken boards, and saws, but they just didn't seem suitable. Then I found my husband's old tool belt, and got an idea. I asked him if he would be my model, and wear the tool belt so I could take a picture. Reluctantly, he agreed to let me snap a few pictures, so I did it as fast as I possibly could before he grew impatient with me.

When I first saw the picture, I dismissed it right away because it was dull and boring, but I kept coming back to it for some odd reason. There was just something about that picture that intrigued me, so I decided to put it in *Lightroom 4* to see how I could play around with it. Am I ever glad I did because the moment I played around with the lighting and shadows, the photo started to pop and I could picture the ebook cover exactly.

I won't show you the before and after because both are very similar, but basically I simply changed the lighting and shadows and took out the green.

Here's the final product.

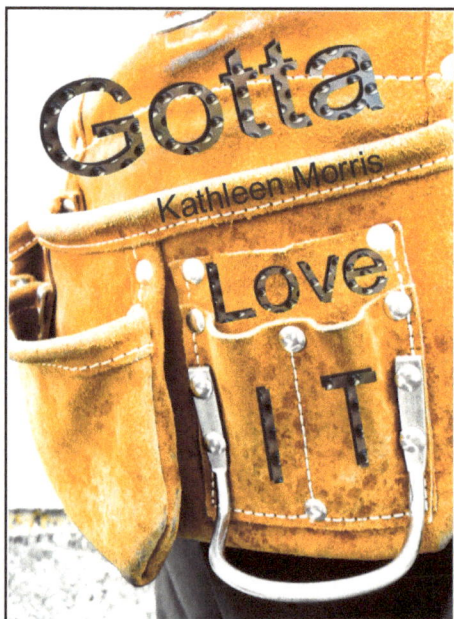

The bottom of the picture used to be green. That was the grass. I found it very distracting. Sometimes you just have to go with only two colors. Don't confuse the reader. Draw their eye to one main thing. And that was the tool belt. All I had to do was remove the green hue and change the shadow to darker. You can do this in *Lightroom 4* or any other photo editing software.

Naturally, the lettering fit like a glove inside the pockets just like the shorts. And I was able to use a font that actually looked like metal. I think it gives it a unique striking look and one that draws the eye to it immediately, even in a thumbnail. In fact, draining the green out, leaving grey/silver and rust as the main colors, helps one focused on the title.

So, don't ever dismiss particular props because of what they are. Who would've known that my husband's workshop would have such lovely gems inside. But there are many things that you can photograph, from jewellery to tools. Experiment with everything and you'll find your ebook cover. You will have original, never seen before, eye-catching ebook covers that won't infringe copyright laws, or draw you into a lawsuit for using someone else's picture, because you own the copyright, and it won't cost you an arm and leg to do it. Now, that is worth its weight in gold.

SAMPLE 2

USING SHADOW TO YOUR ADVANTAGE

A good example of using shadow in an ebook cover, is my latest novel called *The Prion Attachment* - my zombie thriller. Right away, I knew what I wanted to represent my book. I just didn't know exactly how I was going to portray it, so I tried several different things. I wanted my own hand to be a focal point, so I tried taking a picture of it against different backgrounds and didn't like any of them.

It's a Christian story about bondage, so I figured I'd use chains to represent it somehow. I didn't want to do much mucking around, so I wanted another all-in-one with very little editing. I needed props in layers. I wanted light to play a key factor in the photo and decided I'd play with that, rather than color or special effects.

I muddied up my hand, getting dirt deep into my fingernails, and smeared ketchup and Soya sauce on my hand to represent infected blood. It worked wonderfully. I then tied a large chain to my kitchen cupboard, and held onto the end, as a beam of light shone through my skylight against the chain.

I took photos with my other hand and snapped away. I usually turn my camera vertically when I take pictures for ebooks, because then I can use the picture straight out of the camera rather than horizontally, without having to crop it or play around with the canvas. With this particular photo, turning the camera vertically presented quite a challenge considering the awkward position my other hand was in. But *can't* isn't in my vocabulary.

Here is my final ebook cover.

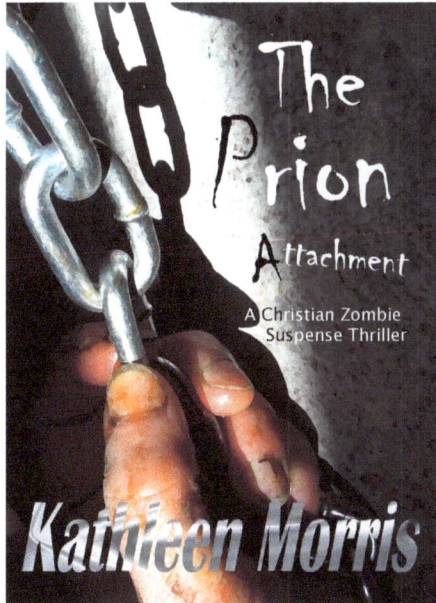

As you can see, the hand turned out quite nicely as it holds the chain against the backsplash, against my kitchen countertop in the sunlight. The grey and white speckled countertop goes with the grey and the black silvers in the photo, drawing the eye to the neutral hand as a focal point.

By using lighting in this way, it created an unexpected shadow for the chain which adds to the appeal of the cover. It also represents change from within, and that is what the story is all about. It also represents what a *Prion* is, and shows how it ultimately attaches to a virus, causing a world wide pandemic. By the way, in case you're wondering, this isn't your normal zombie book, and it's quite an unusual genre.

The important lesson here, is using light to your advantage to cast shadows and create images that may not be visible with the naked eye. The key is to play around with light, shadows, natural light, and artificial light. It can make the dullest photo an eye-catching ebook cover.

CHAPTER 6

IT DOESN'T HAVE TO BE HUMAN

SAMPLE 1

USING YOUR PET

I just wanted to briefly touch on the subject and say that the key to making eye-catching ebook covers is utilizing everything you have including your own pet. For one of my plays titled, *Even Me - A Christmas Play For Your Sunday School*, which is about a skunk, I was at a loss for ideas. I didn't want to buy a picture of a skunk from an online site, so I decided to use my own dog. Crazy right? Everyone else calls her ugly, so I figured I could use her as a model to see if she might look like a skunk. Well to me she did, and it worked perfectly. All I had to do was add a border, change the coloring, play with the shadows, and intensify the eye color.

Here is what I came up with.

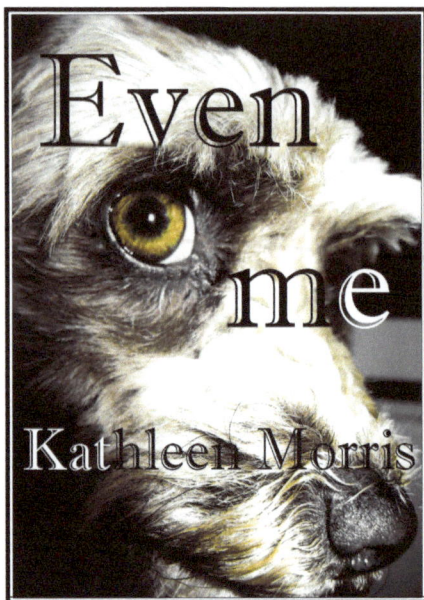

My little dog did a great job at modelling, and makes a perfect skunk.

Here is another example of using your pet. My daughter's dog loves big sticks and it fit perfectly with one of my ebooks called, *Short End Of The Stick*.

Take a look.

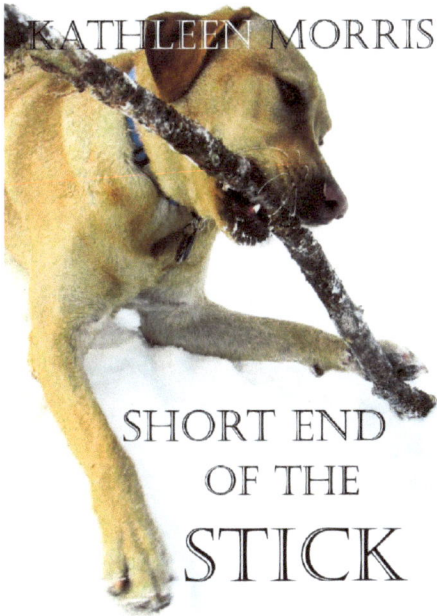

Notice how I utilized the free space to add the title. Whenever you find that a picture has some empty space, that's where your title goes. Balance it according to the photo, center it if necessary, and make it look like it belongs there. That's how you make eye-catching ebook covers, easily.

CHAPTER 7

LESS IS MORE

SAMPLE 1

FONT EFFECT

When I thought about the image I wanted for this ebook cover, I knew I wanted something simple, so I went for an eye. Not just any eye, but *my* eye. Yes, I almost blinded myself taking a picture of my multi-colored eye. It's unique, and that's what I wanted for my cover. Ebook covers should be unique and stand out. A boring stock photo that someone else might use, is not going to stand out. You want unusual, different, unique pictures, that scream *buy me*.

I had to take dozens of pictures of my eye to get the exact color and look I was going for. I wanted to have a lot of shadow in the picture so I made sure my flash was on as I stood in front of the window. The result was amazing. I used *Lightroom 4* to take out all the color. It has an *HSL* feature that you can play with to remove individual colors and then put back the way you want. I then clicked on the brush feature and brushed in the colors on my pupil.

Of course, as I stated before, any photo editing software can do the same thing as *Lightroom 4*. You just have to learn how to use it. Changing, removing, and brushing colors on, is something all photo editing software can do.

Once I found the exact image I wanted to use, I tried several different fonts for the title. It took me a long time before settling for the font I went with, and the process was gruelling. At first I had the title sideways, then top and bottom, then I brought it together. But, it just didn't look right. I made several different samples and saved them. I always went back the next morning to check if I liked it but I never did.

Finally, I decided to start from scratch with the fonts. I realized because my ebook had a long title, I couldn't clutter the cover up with big gonky fonts. That's what I was doing up to this point. I had too much going on. Instead of the big crazy font I had chosen, I decided that less was more. I went with a narrow plain looking font, added a text box and that was it. When I saw the final product, I was in awe. It struck me right away. I always say go with your gut. You'll know when you have it right. Trust yourself. You can do it.

Here is my final cover.

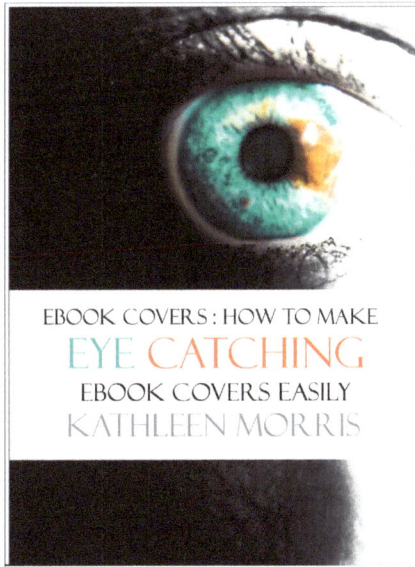

EBOOK COVERS : HOW TO MAKE
EYE CATCHING
EBOOK COVERS EASILY
KATHLEEN MORRIS

As you can see, the simple font, even though I added some color, takes attention away from the title and brings it to the eye, which was what I was going for. Less really is more.

CHAPTER 8

FIXING PROBLEMS

I could go on and on using several other ebook covers as examples, but this ebook would be far too long and I think that you've got the point in most areas. There is however one more sample I would like to show you, and that is an ebook cover I was commissioned to do that took quite a while because of some problems. The author wanted to make her own prop, a picture of an eye, that went with the sci-fi fantasy book she had written. It was quite unique, and I struggled with it for a while before I figured out what to do with it. The picture had not been taken in *Macro*, so it was a challenge to work with because it was slightly blurred. But I would not give up until I found the solution.

I want to show you what I had to work with before edits, exactly how I received it from the author. This is the raw image as it came out of the camera.

SAMPLE 1

WORKING WITH BLUR

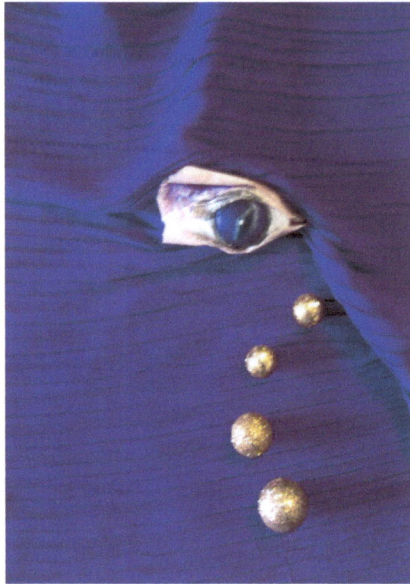

You can't really see it here, but there is a slight blur to the eye, and it was difficult to use this photo, though it's very unique. I just want to point out that even if you can't take a clear picture as well as the next person, or your camera messes up, there is still no reason that you can't make an eye-catching ebook cover. Just don't give up. Try working with it, see what you can do with special effects.

Now originally I wanted to try and fix the blur, but when I tried, it seemed to make it too grainy, and that looked fake to me. And remember, if it looks fake to you, it will look fake to potential readers, and they won't buy it.

So, after a lot of trial and error, I found that working with another picture and layering them together hid the blur, or at the very least made it look like it belonged. I layered it with the following picture.

This is a picture I took through a decorative glass plate as I held it up against the window. A very unique effect. I merged the picture with the one above, and that's called layering. It takes a while to learn how to do this with any kind of software, but if that's what you want to do, then do it. It is something that gives quite an original affect to make an eye-catching ebook cover.

Here is the result.

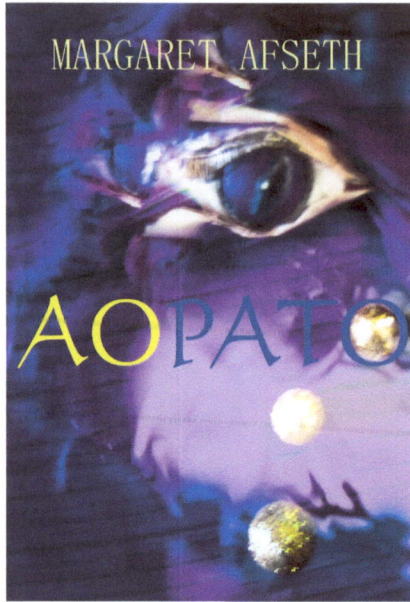

(A special thanks to author Margaret Afseth for the use of her cover in this book. You can find her Sci-fi Fantasy novels on Amazon.com)

As you can see, the two pictures layered together create an eye-catching effect, and intrigue the buyer to wonder what it's about. Notice how the title incorporates the first gold object into its last letter. Use whatever you need to make it look like it belongs together. That is how ebook covers catch the eye. This particular one represents a new species called the *Aopato* people. Quite ingenious actually, especially if you're a sci-fi fantasy fan.

I just want to remind you that layering is a feature that you can add to *Lightroom 4* or access in *Gimp*. Essentially it is up to you when choosing photo software. They all seem to do the same thing in one way or the other, and in my opinion, there isn't one better than the other. After all, you don't want to become a professional photographer, you just want to edit your photos so you can make ebook covers easily. I know that's what I wanted, and I can achieve that with any kind of photo software.

I would suggest whatever type of software you decide to go with, you spend the time learning how to use it. The worst thing in the world is trying to make an ebook cover with software that you don't understand. You'll give up then. Don't give up! Instead, learn what you need to learn and move on quickly.

CHAPTER 9

THE DO'S AND DON'TS

There are many rules you want to follow to achieve the best eye-catching ebook covers, easily. Included in those rules are the do's and don'ts.

THE DO'S

- *Use your own digital camera* (no need to go out and buy a fancy new expensive one. Even something with a low pixel count like 8 pixels will work)
- *Always use the Macro feature* (and if you don't know where that feature is on your camera, go through your instruction booklet now and find it)
- *Trial and error* (take a lot of pictures, and don't be afraid to try)
- *When you don't succeed, try, try again!*
- *Use photo editing software, free versions if possible*
- *Use different kinds of props, even the strange ones*
- Use your pets as models
- Use your friends and family as models

- Layer your photos
- Make all-in-one photos
- Play with shadows
- Change colors
  - Play around with fonts
  - Sleep on it (leave the picture overnight, take a look at it the next morning. It will do wonders)
  - Follow the guidelines for Smashwords and Amazon Kindle for ebook covers

THE DON'TS

- Don't listen to them when they say you need to hire a professional ebook cover designer. You can do it all by yourself!

- Don't give up (this is a given)

- Don't bold your title font (just use the fonts available)

- Don't use a photo that looks fake or childish (If it looks fake to you, it will look fake to a potential reader, and they won't buy your ebook)

- Don't use a blurry picture (If you have to, then layer it and disguise the blur)

- Don't draw your own picture for an ebook cover. Use a photo (I find that drawings don't catch the eye as much as photos do)

- Don't expect to get the perfect picture in one shot

- Don't let people convince you not to do this

- Don't forget to use Macro

- Don't purchase expensive photo editing software

- You don't need special ebook cover making software

- Don't forget to use free photo editing software

- Did I mention, don't give up? DON'T GIVE UP!

CONCLUSION

I'm no expert, but I know what I look for when searching for my next read. I know what stands out to me, and I know what I bypass. I know what has worked for me in making my own ebook covers, and what has worked for commissioned work as well.

I hope that you will take the information you have learnt from this ebook, and use it to make your own professional eye-catching ebook covers. If this ebook can help anyone even a little bit, it was worth the effort of this author.

I talk to so many self-published indie authors who struggle with making their own ebook covers, thinking their only solution is to dole out the money to commercial artists to make them look professional. This infuriates me. Why make an author feel like they have to do something a certain way before it's so-called professional. This has happened far too long. For years, centuries, the author has been shut out. The publishing industry told us we couldn't self publish our work because it would cheapen it. I don't know how long I believed this lie, but the truth is now out there. We can independently published our writing now thanks to new platforms like Smashwords, Amazon, Apple, Kobo, Barnes & Noble, *and the list goes on. For the first time ever, we writers now have a platform thanks to ebooks. We are the new generation of publishing. We are the independents. We don't need the publishing houses to okay our work before it can be published anymore. We can bypass all that stuff and do it independently. Why on earth would we want to then hire somebody to do the cover? With a little effort and know-how, you can make your own professional eye-catching ebook covers, easily.*

Go independent all the way my fellow writers! You can do ebook covers by yourself and it won't cheapen it. Don't believe the lie that you can't. If anyone tries to tell you otherwise, stand up for yourself and say, "Don't tell me what I can or cannot do! I'm an indie author!"

Now get busy and make that ebook cover!

The End

ABOUT THE AUTHOR

Award-winning author Kathleen Morris has written numerous articles, poetry, and short stories published in various Saskatchewan newspapers. Her poem Refuge is published in a book anthology titled A Golden Morning. She has written many plays and skits including her play titled Gotta Love It, winner of Dancing Sky Theatre's rural writing contest in 2001 where it was also performed by the theatre troupe in Meacham, Saskatchewan.

Deep Bay Vengeance is Kathleen's first novel followed by its sequel Deep Bay Relic. She also writes non-fiction inspirational books about funny stories from her own life. Her latest novel is called The Prion Attachment, first book in the Blood War Series. When she's not writing, she enjoys spending time with her husband Barry and their three grown children at her home in Saskatchewan, Canada. For more on Kathleen Morris please check out her Amazon Author Page on Amazon.com.

BOOKS BY KATHLEEN MORRIS

Bay Series
Deep Bay Vengeance
Deep Bay Relic
Deep Bay Legacy (Coming 2014)

Blood War Series
The Prion Attachment
Blood Purge (Coming 2014)

Short Inspirations Series
Size Seven Shorts
Short End Of The Stick
Shortcut To Alaska

Short Stories
Along The Way - 12 Short Stories You Can Read Along
The Way

Plays
Time Will Tell - An Easter Play
Even Me - A Christmas Play For Your Sunday School
All I Need Is Love - A Play For Teens
Lost And Found - A Children's Christmas Play
Gotta Love It - A Humorous Play About Rural Life

How - To Books
How To Make Eye Catching Ebook Covers Easily

Available on Amazon.com